50 Fun-Filled
SPANISH
DRAW & WRITE
PROMPTS

by Alyse Sweeney

S C H O L A S T I C
PROFESSIONAL**B**OOKS

NEW YORK • TORONTO • LONDON • AUCKLAND • SYDNEY
MEXICO CITY • NEW DELHI • HONG KONG • BUENOS AIRES

82989

Cover design by Norma Ortiz
Interior illustrations by James Graham Hale
Interior design by Solutions by Design, Inc.
Translated by Susana Pasternac

ISBN: 0-439-49869-4

Contents

Introduction

Welcome to *50 Fun-Filled Spanish Draw & Write Prompts*! These appealing reproducible pages pair drawing prompts with quick companion writing prompts on topics kids know and love: favorite animals, friends, family members, special events, playtime, school, and more. Each page invites children to create a drawing about a topic before putting their ideas into words. Kids love to draw because it gives them the freedom to express themselves creatively. As a pre-writing warm-up, drawing sparks kids' interest, helps them generate ideas and details for writing, and makes their subjects lively and real.

The variety of fun formats in this book encourages children to produce varied types of writing: personal, interactive, informative, and creative. Beginning writers flourish when given the opportunity to write about topics that are important to them and that they know about. Through personal writing, kids draw upon their own experiences, surroundings, and preferences. Interactive writing, such as Draw & Write Greeting Cards, fosters relationships with others. Children are able to show what they know about various topics through informative writing. In Color & Write and Connect the Dots & Write, children first discover a hidden picture and then use prior knowledge to write about topics such as animals, ice cream, and sports. Students also produce creative writing when they write stories about various animals and their own imaginary creature.

50 Fun-Filled Spanish Draw & Write Prompts provides students with fun and motivating opportunities to write, and also helps children recognize that they have something worthwhile to say. Giving children opportunities to share their writing helps them gain confidence as writers. It also allows them to build fluency and develop their reading skills. Encourage children to share their Draw & Write Prompts both at school and at home. Family members will particularly enjoy "Mi familia" on page 24 and any of the Draw & Write Greeting Cards on pages 38–43.

50 Fun-Filled Spanish Draw & Write Prompts engages beginning writers of all ability levels. So jump right in and watch your students develop enthusiasm and confidence as writers!

How to Use This Book

The reproducible Draw & Write pages are grouped together by format (bookmarks, charts, interviews, and so on). You can use the pages in any order. You'll find that Draw & Write Prompts are easy to integrate into your curriculum. For example, Draw & Write All About Me pages are perfect for getting to know one another at the beginning of the school year; "Animales extraordinarios" on page 25 ties in nicely with a unit on animal studies; and Draw & Write Cartoons enhance character education. You'll find specific suggestions for using each prompt on pages 6–11.

Pre-Writing

Choose a Draw & Write page and make enough copies for your class. Set the stage for writing by discussing the topic. A pre-writing discussion helps students activate prior knowledge. Then give each child a copy of the reproducible page, crayons, and pencils. Read the directions aloud and show students where to draw on the page. As children are drawing, encourage them to add details that may later help them in their writing.

After students have finished with their drawings, you may wish to give them an opportunity to talk about what they have drawn. They can describe their drawing to you, a partner, a small group, or the whole class. This will also help them generate ideas for their writing.

Writing

Read the prompts aloud so that children are clear about what they will be writing. The prompts are easily adapted to different levels of writing development. You may wish to brainstorm as a class a list of possible responses and write them on chart paper or on the chalkboard. When students are writing, they can refer to the list for ideas or for help with spelling. Children can also refer to the word banks on many pages to guide them as they are writing.

Sharing

Children will experience many benefits when they share their writing with their classmates, teachers, families, and others. When children share their writing, they see themselves as writers, develop reading skills, and build fluency. And because the prompts capture the thoughts, experiences, and interests of the writer, they provide a tremendous opportunity for students to get to know one another. Children will see that there are things they have in common with others and that each person is a unique individual.

Collaborative Class Books

When students have completed their prompt page, bind the pages together to make a collaborative class book about that topic. Invite a student to decorate a cover, and then add the book to your classroom library. Have students take turns bringing home the book in a resealable plastic bag to share with family members.

Getting Started With
Draw & Write Prompts

DRAW & WRITE BOOKMARKS

Draw & Write Bookmarks are a great way to motivate kids to read. The three bookmarks invite children to draw and then generate a list related to their picture. Lists are an important writing format that can help children organize ideas for writing. When children have completed their bookmarks, they can use their lists to generate longer, more detailed pieces.

"Yo puedo..." marca páginas

Brainstorm with children a list of things that they can do. Students may know how to play a certain game, write stories, help a parent cook dinner, or draw a shark. Ask students to think about how they learned these skills. Did someone teach them? Did they practice and learn on their own? Lead a discussion about things students would like to learn how to do. Make a list on chart paper for students to refer to during the year. They can write their initials beside skills on the list as they learn them.

"A mí me gusta..." marca páginas

As a class, generate a list of activities that children like to do. Encourage children to think about things they like to do at school, at home, in after-school programs, at camp, or elsewhere. They may like to play soccer, write poems, read to a sibling, or play with a pet. Elicit from children reasons why they like to do these activities. For example, do they like to play soccer because they like to run, be outside, spend time with their teammates, or all three?

"Me gusta leer sobre..." marca páginas

Brainstorm with children lists of topics they like to read about. Direct their attention to the illustration on the page and to books around the classroom for ideas. They may like to read about planets, animals, friends, families, funny things, sports, and so on. Ask children to think about books that they read at home as well.

If you have students who tend to read the same books or same types of books, this bookmark may help them expand their reading preferences. Hearing what their classmates like to read about may also motivate them to try new books or topics.

DRAW & WRITE ALL ABOUT ME

Each page in this section focuses on an aspect of children's immediate world, enabling them to write about who they are. The writing format is straightforward and the pages provide generous space for drawing. These prompts are a great way for children to learn about one another at the beginning of the year. When students have completed all nine pages in this section, they can assemble the pages and make a cover for an All About Me book.

Mis manos/Mis pies

Ask children to think about the many things that they can do with their hands and feet. Have them think about how they use their hands and feet both in and out of school (writing, painting, running, jumping, and so on). Children can use the word bank on each page to help them as they are writing.

50 Fun-Filled Spanish Draw & Write Prompts Scholastic Professional Books

For an extension, have children trace their hands and feet on colored paper and cut out the outlines. Ask them to write an action word in the outline that is something they can do with either their hands or their feet. Display them on a bulletin board.

Mis dientes

Children will need small unbreakable mirrors to draw a picture of their smile. After they draw their smile, they will record how many teeth they have lost so far. Emphasize that children should not worry or be upset if they have not lost any teeth yet. They will soon! Brainstorm as a group why teeth are important. Ask students to think about how difficult it would be to eat without teeth. Ask them what sorts of food babies eat and why.

¡A comer!

After children draw their favorite foods on the large plate on this page, they write about their food preferences. Have children share one food they like and one food they dislike as a pre-writing warm-up. This page ties in well with a study of nutrition. Lead a discussion about what kinds of foods are nutritious, and ask children if the food they drew is nutritious.

Mi juguete favorito

Encourage students to use details in both their drawing and their written description of their favorite toy. Model for the class a detailed description of a toy by telling about your favorite toy when you were a child. When students have completed their Draw & Write page, they can play "20 Questions" to guess one another's toys. They can ask questions such as, "Is your toy soft?" or "Does it have wheels?"

Mi cuarto

On this page, children draw a picture of their room and write about what they do there. Have children brainstorm the activities that they do in their rooms, such as sleep, play with toys, read, write, and get dressed. Encourage children to use the details in their drawing to help them as they are writing. As an extension, discuss the activities that typically take place in other rooms of a home.

Jugar al aire libre/ Jugar adentro

What are your students' favorite outdoor and indoor activities? On these pages, they'll draw and then write about playing outside and inside. Have a discussion about how the weather and seasons affect what types of games your students play. What do they play when it is warm? Cold? Rainy? Snowy?

Mi amigo, _____

Have children write their friend's name on the line in the title. Then invite them to draw a picture of their friend. As a class, generate a list of words that describe friends. Encourage students to think about what activities they like to do with their friend at school or at home. This page can lead into a discussion about what makes a good friend and how children can be good friends to others.

DRAW & WRITE CHARTS

Draw & Write Charts give students an opportunity to write about their family, favorite animals, and favorite books in a chart format. Charts require students to cluster, or categorize, information. This is a helpful organizational skill for students to use in their writing. Model for children how to fill in a chart before they begin.

After children have completed these three charts, have them create their own charts. Help them choose a broad topic such as favorite foods, activities, games, places, and so on.

Mi familia

Ask students to choose family members to draw and then write about. Encourage children to consider extended relatives, such as grandparents, aunts, uncles, and cousins.

Show students the line in each box on which to write the family member's name. This is a nice send-home activity that family members will enjoy reading.

Animales extraordinarios

This chart works well as a pre-writing activity for an animal report. Children choose two of their favorite animals to draw; then they write one interesting fact and one thing they would like to learn about each animal. When children complete their chart, have them research the fact that they wanted to know.

Mis libros favoritos

For this chart, children choose two of their favorite books to draw. In the space provided, they can draw the book cover or a character or scene from the book. Children then write a sentence stating what each book is about and a sentence describing their favorite part of each book. This chart is a good introduction to writing a simple book report because it requires specific and succinct information. Have children use their charts to write or dictate a book report on one of their books. Display the charts in your classroom or school library to help students make book selections.

DRAW & WRITE SEQUENCING

In this section, students write the steps to do three everyday activities. As they draw and write about each step, children develop important sequencing skills.

When students have finished these pages, make a sequencing game about one of the activities (brushing teeth, getting ready for bed, and so on). Write each step on an index card. Working with partners, students read the cards and arrange the steps in order. For younger students, draw a picture on each card to guide their reading.

Me lavo los dientes

Begin by discussing the steps involved in brushing teeth. It is helpful to bring in a toothbrush and toothpaste and demonstrate the steps for children. Have students choose four steps and draw each one in a box. The steps can be very simple, such as "Put toothpaste on my toothbrush, brush my teeth, rinse my mouth," and so on. This activity ties in nicely with a unit on health.

Vamos a dormir/ Vamos a la escuela

Begin by having your students share the steps they take to get ready for bed and to get ready for school. Students can organize their writing in a graphic organizer as a pre-writing warm-up. You may wish to model this for students first.

DRAW & WRITE INTERVIEWS

There are two parts to each Draw & Write Interview. On the first page, children draw a picture about a specified topic and write about it. On the second page, children draw themselves beside an interviewer. Students read the interviewer's question in the speech balloon and write a response in their own speech balloon. Cartoons and speech balloons are highly motivating to children and help them visualize the interview. There are additional interview questions below each cartoon. You may wish to show students examples of comic strips so that they will better understand how speech balloons work. As an extension, have students conduct interviews with each other or with students in other classes. As a group, think of topics for the interviews and generate questions. Students can interview their partner in front of the class or in front of a small group.

Mi escuela/Mi entrevista sobre mi escuela

After students draw a picture of their school, ask them to look at their drawings to help them think of words that describe their school. What is their favorite place at school: the library, cafeteria, playground, or elsewhere? Finally, have them think of one special thing about their school. Remind them that it can be anything: a special person, event, place, or even the feeling that they get when they are at school. On the interview page, show students where to draw themselves in the cartoon. Help them read the interviewer's question and explain that they should write a response in the speech balloon. Then have them respond to the additional interview questions below the cartoon.

¡Feliz Halloween!/ Mi entrevista de Halloween

Students begin by drawing something they like to do on Halloween and then writing about it. On the next page, they draw themselves in their Halloween costume next to the interviewer. If children do not yet know what they will be for Halloween, they can draw what they would like to be for Halloween or what they were last year. Ask students to think about why they chose their costume. Is the costume scary or funny? Is it different than last year or the same? Encourage them to use their pictures to decide what is their favorite part of their costume.

Mi animal favorito/ Mi entrevista sobre mi animal favorito

After students draw a picture of their favorite animal, have them answer the questions about the animal's size, color, habitat, and so on. This activity can lead into a mini-report about their animal. On the next page, children draw themselves being interviewed by a zookeeper about their favorite animal. Ask students to think about why they like this animal so much. Is it because it can do cool things, like change colors or catch insects with its tongue? If children have trouble answering the last question about an interesting fact, help them find a fact in a book or encourage them to write about a physical characteristic.

Mi lugar favorito/ Mi entrevista sobre mi lugar favorito

Students begin by drawing a picture of their favorite place and writing about it. If they have trouble thinking of a place, work together to list places in your community, such as a park, library, public pool, or skating rink. On the next page, students draw themselves beside the interviewer and respond to questions about their favorite place. As a follow-up, ask children where they would like to visit that they have not been to before?

DRAW & WRITE GREETING CARDS

With Draw & Write Greeting Cards, children write and decorate cards for special people in their lives. This helps children see that the written language can be used to reach out and connect to other people. Discuss with children about how nice it feels to receive cards and how they will be making other people happy by sending them. Children can hand deliver their cards, but it is also fun to mail them. Model for children how to address an envelope and where to put the stamp. You can also set up a mail station in your classroom with a mailbox for each student. Leave supplies in the station for children to send letters and cards to their classmates. As an extension, children may want to make and send cards to people in hospitals or nursing homes. Greeting cards from your students are a great way to bring cheer to others in the community.

For each of the six Draw & Write Greeting Cards, show students how to fold the paper to assemble the card (directions appear on the card). Have children draw a picture related to the card in the box on the front. On the inner left side of the card, have children respond to the short writing prompt. The writing prompts on the inner right side are more open-ended. You may wish to brainstorm possible messages with children before they begin writing. If children have extra time, encourage them to draw a picture on the back of the card as well.

Send home Draw & Write Greeting Cards for Thanksgiving, winter holidays, and Valentine's Day. Keep extra copies on hand of the Thank You card, Happy Birthday card, and Congratulations card. Encourage children to make these cards for classmates and family members whenever the occasion arises.

DRAW & WRITE CARTOONS

Draw & Write Cartoons encourage children to think about how to resolve conflicts peacefully. The speech balloons and cartoons generate children's interest and prompt them to think about how they would respond in that situation. Draw & Write Cartoons are ideal for lessons on character education.

As an extension, children can share their completed Draw & Write Cartoons by role-playing with a partner. Role-playing these situations is also an excellent way for your students to develop and practice conflict-resolution skills.

Compartamos

Read the speech balloon aloud and ask children to think about how they would feel if someone asked for something in the way David did. Have students think about how they can respond nicely to David. Invite them to draw themselves in the box and write their response in the speech balloon. Ask children to think of how David might have asked for the crayon in a nicer way, such as, "May I use that crayon when you are done?" or "Please tell me when you are done with that crayon so that I can use it." They can write additional responses on the back of the page.

Hagamos las paces

Read the speech balloon aloud with your class. Ask students to think about how they would feel if someone broke their toy. What do they think the other person could say to make them feel better? What kind of responses would make them feel worse, such as "So!" or "I don't care." Next have students draw themselves in the cartoon and write in the speech balloon what they would say to Sara to make her feel better. Responses may include, "I'm sorry," "Let me help you glue it together," or "I didn't mean to break your toy. It was an accident."

Juguemos juntos

Have students draw themselves in the cartoon playing a game. Ask them how they think the child that is left out feels. What would they say if their friend asked if he or she could play also? Responses may include, "I'm going to ask my friend to play with us," or "Let's invite my friend to play too."

¡Resuelve un problema!

On this page, children make up a situation in which two children are having a problem. Then, they write down their solution. Guide children through this exercise by reminding them of conflicts that were resolved peacefully in the classroom or on the playground. Or, brainstorm together areas of the classroom where potential conflicts may take place, such as a computer station where children have to take turns. This open-ended activity works well as a follow-up to the other Draw & Write Cartoons.

COLOR & WRITE

In this section, children color by number to discover a hidden object in each picture. They then use prior knowledge to write about what they know about the object. The word bank guides children to write factual information, making this section a good introduction to report writing.

Read the instructions aloud with your students. Emphasize that they are asked to write three facts about flowers. Model the difference between fact and opinion. For example, "I think flowers are pretty" states an opinion, whereas "Flowers come in many colors" states a fact. Similarly, "I had ice cream last night" is a personal statement, whereas "Ice cream is cold, but can melt fast" shows what the child knows about ice cream.

As an extension, have children produce personal writing on one of the topics. For example, students may write about their favorite flavor of ice cream, where they have eaten ice cream, or an ice cream cake they once had at a birthday. Have students share both pieces of writing with the class. Discuss the different type of information given in each piece.

CONNECT THE DOTS & WRITE

In this section, children will enjoy connecting the dots to reveal animal drawings: a spider, a starfish, and a pair of monkeys. After they discover the animals, children answer questions about them. Children can make their own connect-the-dot surprises by drawing a picture in light pencil and then adding dots and numbers in pen or marker. When the ink has dried, they can erase the pencil. Have children trade their connect-the-dot pictures with a partner and complete them. Then they can write or narrate a short story about the pictures.

DRAW & WRITE STEP BY STEP

Each of these Draw & Write prompts has two pages. The first page shows how to draw an animal in six easy steps. It is a good idea to give children scrap paper on which to practice drawing the steps. Remind children that the steps are only a guide; children can draw the animal in their own style if they wish. When they are ready, they can draw the animal on the second page and color it. The writing prompts at the bottom of the second page form a fill-in-the-blank creative story. Kids fill in the missing information with their own imaginative ideas. They'll enjoy sharing their stories and hearing how each one is unique.

DRAW & WRITE CREATURES

Children use their imagination to create their own made-up creature. On the first page, they draw the creature in the box and then answer questions about it. The questions will help children organize their thoughts for the writing to come on the next page. Encourage children to think of more questions about their creatures and answer them on the back of the page. This section is a good introduction to pre-writing. On the second page, kids make up a mini-story by drawing four things that happen to their creature. Below each drawing, they write a description of the event. Remind children to refer to their writing on the first page as they are writing their mini-story. This activity can serve as a graphic organizer to write a longer, more detailed story. Depending upon their literacy development, children can either write, dictate, or narrate a story about their creature.

As an extension, have children make three-dimensional versions of their creatures with clay. Display the clay creatures along with children's creative stories.

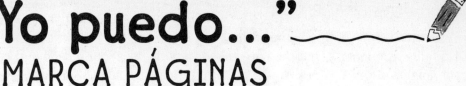

"Yo puedo..."
MARCA PÁGINAS

por _____

Piensa en todas las cosas que puedas hacer.

Dibuja dentro del círculo una cosa que puedes hacer.

Escribe sobre las líneas cuatro cosas que puedas hacer.

Recorta tu marca páginas por la línea de puntos.

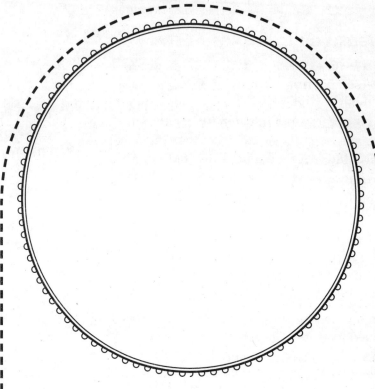

Dibuja dentro del círculo lo que puedes hacer.

Yo puedo _____

_____

Yo puedo _____

_____

Yo puedo _____

_____

Yo puedo _____

_____

50 Fun-Filled Spanish Draw & Write Prompts Scholastic Professional Books

"A mí me gusta..."
MARCA PÁGINAS

por _____

Piensa en todas las cosas que te gusta hacer.

Dibuja dentro del círculo una cosa que te gusta hacer.

Escribe sobre las líneas cuatro cosas que te gusta hacer.

Recorta tu marca páginas por la línea de puntos.

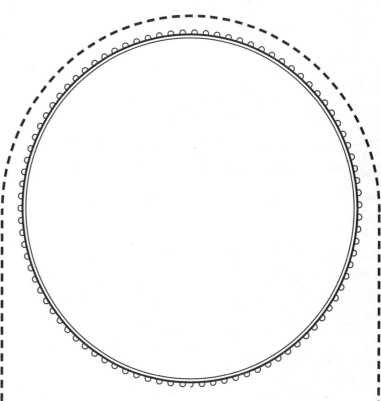

Dibuja dentro del círculo algo que te gusta hacer.

A mí me gusta _____

_____

A mí me gusta _____

_____

A mí me gusta _____

_____

A mí me gusta _____

_____

"Me gusta leer sobre..."
MARCA PÁGINAS

por _____

Piensa en todas las cosas sobre las que te gusta leer.

Dibuja dentro del libro una cosa sobre la que te gusta leer.

Escribe sobre las líneas cuatro cosas sobre las que te gusta leer.

Recorta tu marca páginas por la línea de puntos.

Dibuja dentro del libro algo sobre lo que te gusta leer.

Me gusta leer sobre...

1. _____

_____

2. _____

_____

3. _____

_____

4. _____

_____

14

Mis Manos

por _____

Traza el contorno de tu mano en el recuadro de abajo.

Estas son tres cosas que puedo hacer con mis manos.

Puedo _____

_____

Puedo _____

_____

Puedo _____

_____

BANCO DE PALABRAS

tocar

cosquillear

aplaudir

acariciar

dibujar

señalar

saludar

escribir

Mis pies

por _____

Traza el contorno de tu pie en el recuadro de abajo.

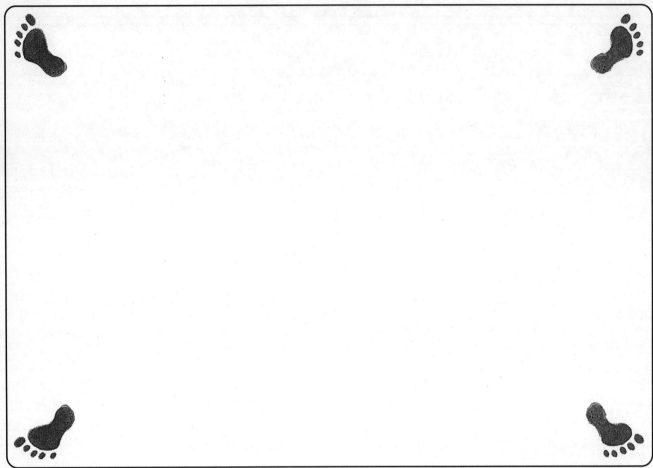

Estas son tres cosas que puedo hacer con mis pies.

Puedo _____

_____

Puedo _____

_____

Puedo _____

_____

50 Fun-Filled Spanish Draw & Write Prompts Scholastic Professional Books

Mis dientes

por _____

Mírate en el espejo para ver cómo son tus dientes. Luego dibuja tu sonrisa en el recuadro de abajo.

Hasta ahora, he perdido _____ dientes.

Estoy contento de tener dientes porque

_____

_____

_____

_____

BANCO DE PALABRAS

masticar

morder

triturar

cortar

comer

mordisquear

moler

¡A comer!

por _____

Dibuja tu comida favorita en el plato.

Me gusta comer _____.

Pero, no me gusta comer _____.

_____ y _____ son sabrosos juntos.

_____ y _____ no son sabrosos juntos.

50 Fun-Filled Spanish Draw & Write Prompts Scholastic Professional Books

Mi juguete favorito

 por _____

Dibuja tu juguete favorito en el recuadro de abajo.

[drawing box]

Mi juguete favorito es _____

Estas son las palabras que describen mi juguete

favorito: _____

_____

Es mi juguete favorito porque

_____

_____

Mi cuarto

 por _____

Dibuja tu cuarto en el recuadro de abajo.

[drawing box]

Estas son las palabras que describen mi cuarto:

_____

_____

Estas son las cosas que hay en mi cuarto:

_____

_____

Esto es algo que a mí me gusta hacer en mi cuarto.

Me gusta _____

_____

BANCO DE PALABRAS

cama

silla

juguetes

libros

ventana

mesa

lámpara

limpio

desordenado

20

Jugar al aire libre

 por _____

En este dibujo estoy yo jugando al aire libre.

¿A qué juegas?

Estoy jugando a _____

Me gusta jugar a eso porque _____

_____

¿Estás jugando solo o con un amigo?

Estoy jugando _____

Jugar adentro

por _____

En este dibujo estoy yo jugando adentro.

```
┌─────────────────────────────────────────────┐
│                                               │
│                                               │
│                                               │
│                                               │
│                                               │
│                                               │
│                                               │
│                                               │
│                                               │
│                                               │
└─────────────────────────────────────────────┘
```

¿A qué juegas?

Estoy jugando a _____

Me gusta jugar a eso porque _____

_____

¿Estás jugando solo o con un amigo?

Estoy jugando _____

Me gusta jugar adentro cuando _____

_____

50 Fun-Filled Spanish Draw & Write Prompts Scholastic Professional Books

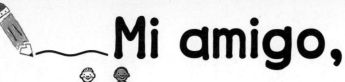

Mi amigo, _____

por _____

Este es el retrato de mi amigo.

```
┌ ─ ─ ─ ─ ─ ─ ─ ─ ─ ─ ─ ─ ─ ─ ─ ─ ─ ─ ─ ┐



│                                       │



└ ─ ─ ─ ─ ─ ─ ─ ─ ─ ─ ─ ─ ─ ─ ─ ─ ─ ─ ─ ┘
```

Estas son las palabras que describen a mi amigo.

_____

_____

Esto es algo que a mi amigo y a mí nos gusta hacer juntos.

Nos gusta _____

Me gusta mi amigo porque _____

_____

Mi familia

por _____

Dibuja a dos personas de tu familia en los recuadros. Escribe el nombre de cada uno de ellos debajo del dibujo. Luego llena la tabla.

Dibuja aquí a dos personas de tu familia.	Esta persona es especial porque...	Lo que me gusta hacer con esta persona es...
_____ nombre		
_____ nombre		

Animales extraordinarios

por _____

Dibuja un animal en cada recuadro. Escribe el nombre de cada animal debajo del dibujo. Luego llena la tabla.

Dibuja al animal aquí.	Algo bueno sobre este animal es...	Lo que me gustaría saber sobre este animal es...
nombre del animal		
nombre del animal		

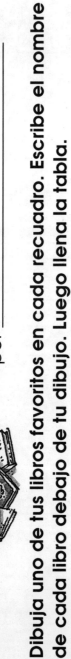

Mis libros favoritos

por _____

Dibuja uno de tus libros favoritos en cada recuadro. Escribe el nombre de cada libro debajo de tu dibujo. Luego llena la tabla.

Haz un dibujo del libro aquí.	Este libro trata de...	La parte que más me gustó de este libro fue...
nombre _____		
nombre _____		

Me lavo los dientes

por _____

¿Cómo te lavas los dientes? Dibuja en estos recuadros los pasos que muestran cómo te lavas los dientes. Luego escribe sobre cada uno de los pasos.

1	2
Primero, yo _____ _____	Después, yo _____ _____
3	**4**
Entonces, yo _____ _____	Por último, yo _____ _____

Vamos a dormir

por _____

¿Cómo te preparas para ir a dormir? Dibuja en los recuadros los pasos que muestran lo que haces para ir a dormir. Luego escribe los diferentes pasos.

1

Primero, yo _____

_____

2

Después, yo _____

_____

3

Entonces, yo _____

_____

4

Por último, yo _____

_____

50 Fun-Filled Spanish Draw & Write Prompts Scholastic Professional Books

Vamos a la escuela

por _____

¿Cómo te preparas para ir a la escuela? Dibuja en los recuadros los pasos que muestran lo que haces para ir a la escuela. Luego escribe los diferentes pasos.

1 Primero, yo _____ _____	**2** Después, yo _____ _____
3 Entonces, yo _____ _____	**4** Por último, yo _____ _____

Mi escuela

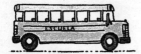

por _____

Dibuja tu escuela en el recuadro de abajo.

[drawing box]

Estas son las palabras que describen mi escuela.

_____

_____

Mi lugar favorito en la escuela es _____

_____

_____

Algo especial sobre mi escuela es _____

_____

_____

50 Fun-Filled Spanish Draw & Write Prompts Scholastic Professional Books

Mi entrevista sobre mi escuela

por _____

Te están entrevistando sobre tu escuela. Lee cada pregunta. Luego escribe tus respuestas sobre las líneas.

¿Qué es lo que más te gusta de tu escuela?

Dibújate aquí. Luego escribe la respuesta en la burbuja.

Entrevistador: ¿Qué estás aprendiendo en la escuela?

Yo: Estoy aprendiendo _____

_____

Entrevistador: ¿Sobre qué cosa te gustaría aprender?

Yo: Me gustaría aprender sobre _____

_____

¡Feliz Halloween!

por _____

Dibuja en la calabaza algo que haces en Halloween.

En este dibujo, yo _____

Me gusta hacer eso porque _____

_____

Lo que más me gusta de Halloween es _____

_____

50 Fun-Filled Spanish Draw & Write Prompts Scholastic Professional Books

Mi entrevista de Halloween

por _____

Te están entrevistando sobre tu disfraz de Halloween. Lee cada pregunta. Luego escribe tus respuestas sobre las líneas.

¿Cuál es tu disfraz?

_____
_____
_____
_____

Dibújate aquí con tu disfraz de Halloween. Luego escribe tu respuesta en la burbuja.

Entrevistador: ¿Por qué elegiste ese disfraz?

Yo: Elegí este disfraz porque _____

_____

Entrevistador: ¿Qué es lo que más te gusta de tu disfraz?

Yo: Lo que más me gusta de mi disfraz es _____

_____

Mi animal favorito

por _____

Dibuja tu animal favorito en el recuadro de abajo.

Mi animal favorito es de color _____

Mi animal favorito es más grande que _____

pero más pequeño que _____

Este es el ruido que mi animal favorito hace: _____

Aquí vive mi animal favorito: _____

_____

34

Mi entrevista sobre mi animal favorito

por _____

Te están entrevistando sobre tu animal favorito. Lee cada pregunta. Luego escribe tus respuestas sobre las líneas.

¿Cuál es tu animal favorito?

_____
_____
_____

Dibújate aquí. Luego escribe tu respuesta en la burbuja.

Guardia de zoológico: ¿Por qué es éste tu animal favorito?

Yo: Es mi animal favorito porque _____

_____

Guardia de zoológico: ¿Qué cosa interesante puedes decir sobre tu animal favorito?

Yo: Una cosa interesante sobre mi animal favorito es _____

_____

Mi lugar favorito

por _____

Dibuja tu lugar favorito en el recuadro de abajo.

```
┌ ─ ─ ─ ─ ─ ─ ─ ─ ─ ─ ─ ─ ─ ─ ─ ─ ┐





│                                 │





│                                 │





└ ─ ─ ─ ─ ─ ─ ─ ─ ─ ─ ─ ─ ─ ─ ─ ─ ┘
```

Mi lugar favorito es _____

Estas son algunas de las cosas que hay en mi lugar favorito: _____

_____

_____

Estas son las palabras que describen mi lugar favorito: _____

_____

_____

50 Fun-Filled Spanish Draw & Write Prompts Scholastic Professional Books

Mi entrevista sobre mi lugar favorito

por _____

Te están entrevistando sobre tu lugar favorito. Lee cada pregunta. Luego escribe tus respuestas sobre las líneas.

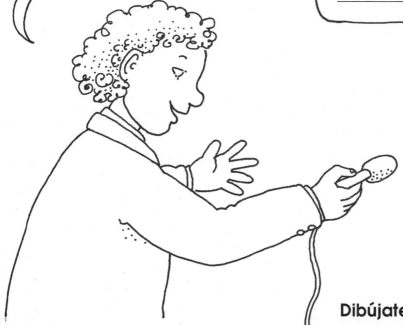

¿Qué te gusta hacer en tu lugar favorito?

_____
_____
_____

Dibújate aquí. Luego escribe tu respuesta en la burbuja.

Entrevistador: ¿Cómo llegas a tu lugar favorito?

Yo: Llego a mi lugar favorito _____

_____

Entrevistador: ¿Por qué es tu lugar favorito?

Yo: Es mi lugar favorito porque _____

_____

¡Hoy cumples ——— años de edad! (Dibuja el número de velitas que te corresponde sobre el pastel.)

De ———

Querido/a ———,
¡Este es mi mensaje de cumpleaños para ti!

1. Primero, dobla por esta línea.

¡Feliz cumpleaños!

2. Después, dobla por esta línea.

(Haz un dibujo en este recuadro.)

Querido/a ______________,

____

____

____

____

____

____

De ______________

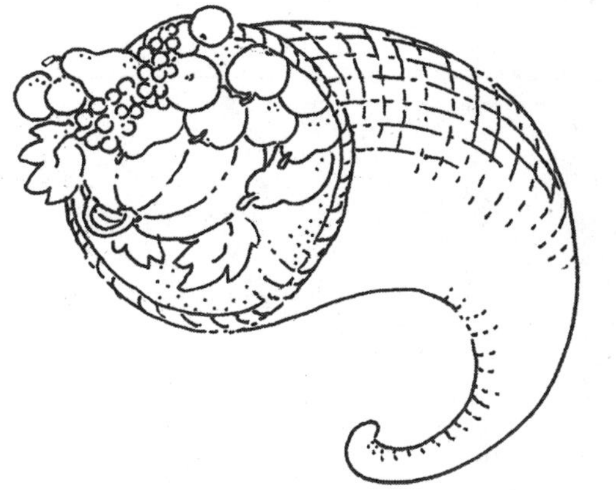

En el Día de Acción de Gracias doy gracias por ______________

____

____

____

1. Primero, dobla por esta línea.

2. Después, dobla por esta línea.

Feliz Día de Acción de Gracias

(Haz un dibujo en este recuadro.)

Las fiestas son especiales porque

____

____

____

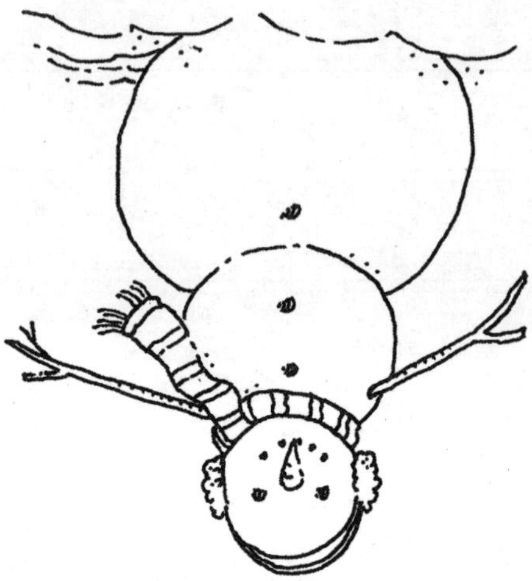

Querido/a ______________,

____

____

____

____

____

De ______________

1. Primero, dobla por esta línea.

¡Felices fiestas!

2. Después, dobla por esta línea.

(Haz un dibujo en este recuadro.)

_____

_____

De _____

_____

_____

_____

_____

_____

Querido/a _____,

_____

_____

Tú eres

1. Primero, dobla por esta línea.

TE QUIERO

YO TE

Feliz Día de la Amistad

2. Después, dobla por esta línea.

(Haz un dibujo en este recuadro.)

De _____

_____

_____

_____

_____

Querido/a _____,

Te agradezco por _____

_____

1. Primero, dobla por esta línea.

¡Gracias!

2. Después, dobla por esta línea.

(Haz un dibujo en este recuadro.)

De _____

_____

_____

_____

_____

_____

_____

Querido/a _____,

_____ Felicitaciones por

_____

1. Primero, dobla por esta línea.

¡Felicitaciones!

2. Después, dobla por esta línea.

(Haz un dibujo en este recuadro.)

Compartamos

por _____

¿Cómo le contestarías a David?

Piensa en una respuesta agradable aunque David no lo haya pedido amablemente.

Dibújate en el recuadro de arriba.

Escribe lo que dirías en la burbuja.

50 Fun-Filled Spanish Draw & Write Prompts Scholastic Professional Books

Hagamos las paces

por _____

¡Rompiste mi juguete!

Imagina que haz roto el juguete de Sara.

¿Qué puedes hacer para que ella se sienta mejor?

Dibújate en el recuadro de arriba.

Luego escribe lo que le dirías en la burbuja.

Juguemos juntos

por _____

Lisa no está jugando contigo.

Dibújate en el recuadro de arriba.

Luego escribe lo que le dirías a Lisa en la burbuja.

50 Fun-Filled Spanish Draw & Write Prompts Scholastic Professional Books

¡Resuelve un problema!

por _____

Dibuja en el recuadro de abajo a dos niños que no se llevan bien.

¿Cuál es el problema que tienen los niños?

_____

_____

¿Qué pueden hacer los niños para resolver su problema? ¿Qué les dirías que hagan?

_____

_____

¡Dulce sorpresa!

por _____

Usa la clave para colorear el dibujo de abajo. ¡Encontrarás una sorpresa muy dulce!

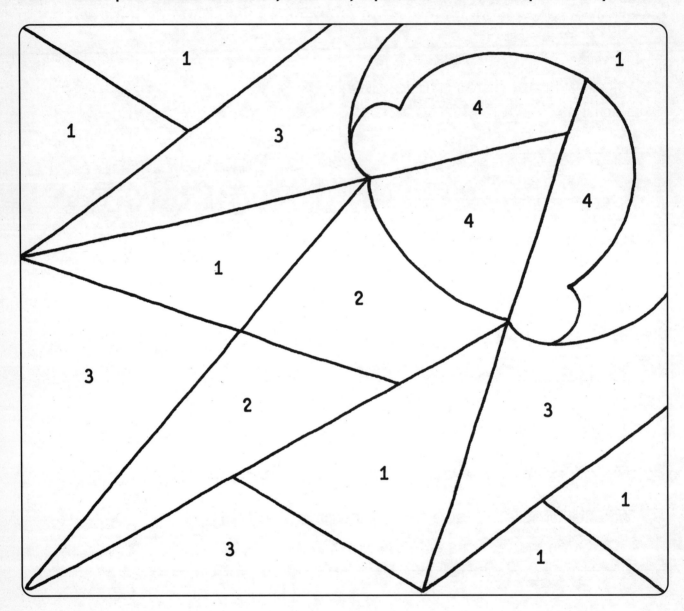

1. rojo

2. marrón

3. verde

4. amarillo

Este es el dibujo de un/una _____

50 Fun-Filled Spanish Draw & Write Prompts Scholastic Professional Books

Todo sobre los helados

por _____

Dibuja el helado más alto que puedas en este recuadro.

Escribe tres cosas que sabes sobre los helados. Si necesitas ayuda, usa las palabras del banco de palabras.

1. _____

_____

2. _____

_____

3. _____

_____

···BANCO DE PALABRAS···

frío	sabroso
sabores	cono
colores	chocolate
derrite	vainilla
dulce	rico

Si pudieras inventar un sabor de helado, ¿de qué sería?

_____

_____

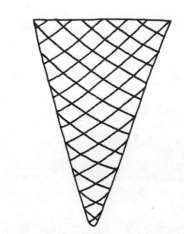

¡Una colorida sorpresa!

por _____

Usa la clave para colorear el dibujo de abajo. ¡Encontrarás una colorida sorpresa!

1. rojo

2. verde

3. amarillo

4. azul

Este es el dibujo de un/una _____

50 Fun-Filled Spanish Draw & Write Prompts Scholastic Professional Books

Todo sobre las flores

por _____

Dibuja unas flores en esta maceta.

Escribe tres cosas que sabes sobre las flores. Si necesitas ayuda, usa las palabras del banco de palabras.

1._____

_____

2._____

_____

3._____

_____

¡Una sorpresa deportiva!

por _____

Usa la clave para colorear el dibujo de abajo. ¡Encontrarás una sorpresa deportiva!

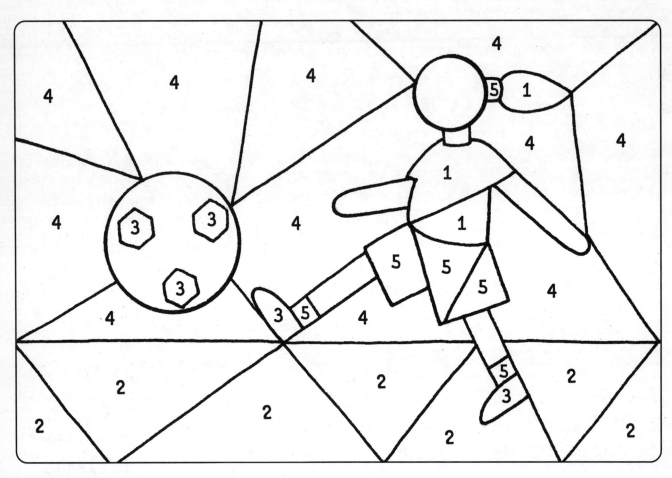

1. amarillo

2. verde

3. negro

4. azul

5. rojo

¿Qué está haciendo la niña en este dibujo? _____

_____

_____

50 Fun-Filled Spanish Draw & Write Prompts Scholastic Professional Books

Mi deporte favorito

por _____

¿Cuál es tu deporte favorito?
Dibújate en el recuadro jugando tu deporte favorito.

[ ]

Escribe tres cosas que sabes sobre tu deporte favorito. Si necesitas ayuda, usa las palabras del banco de palabras.

BANCO DE PALABRAS

1._____

_____

2._____

_____

3._____

_____

gol

equipo

pelota

cancha

pista

correr

puntos

red

jugadores

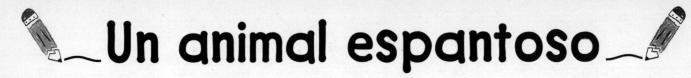

Un animal espantoso

por _____

Conecta los puntos del 1 al 36. Luego contesta las preguntas.

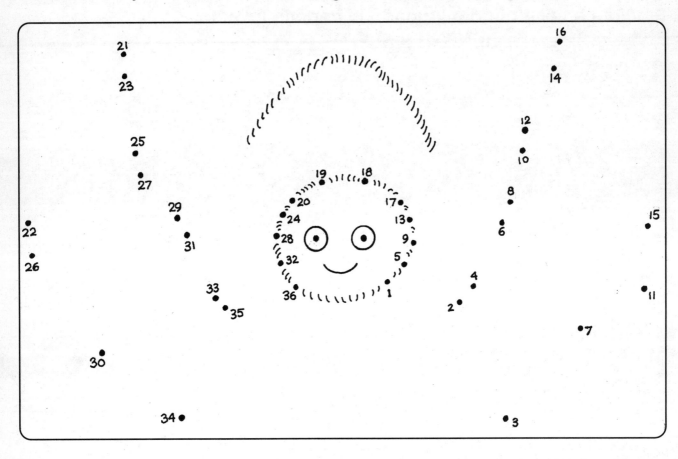

Este animal es _____.

Tiene _____ patas.

Estas son las palabras que describen al animal: _____

_____

¿Te gustaría tener este animal como mascota?

_____

¿Por qué? _____

_____

50 Fun-Filled Spanish Draw & Write Prompts Scholastic Professional Books

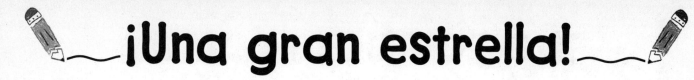

¡Una gran estrella!

por _____

Conecta los puntos del 1 al 31. Luego contesta las preguntas.

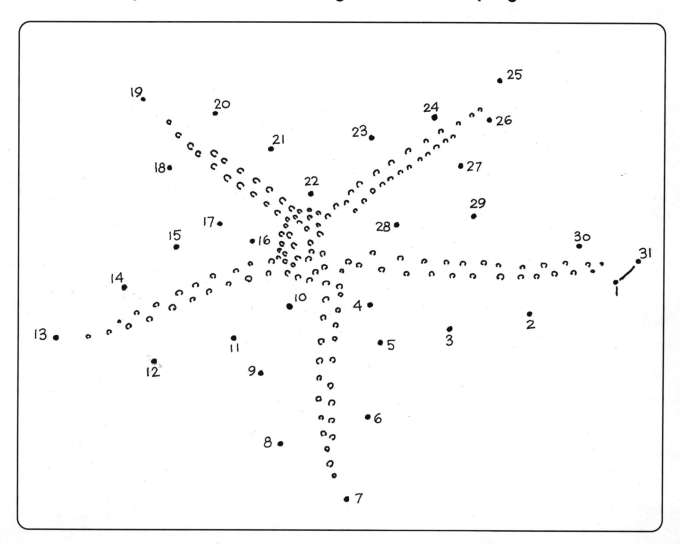

Este animal es _____.

Tiene _____ brazos.

Este animal vive _____

_____

Un hecho interesante sobre este animal es _____

_____

De rama en rama

por_____

Conecta los puntos del 1 al 30. Luego conecta el segundo grupo de puntos del 1 al 31.

Este es el dibujo de _____

_____

Si estos animales pudieran hablar, dirían _____

_____.

Si estos animales fueran tus mascotas, ¿qué nombre les pondrías?

Los llamaría _____ y _____

Un hecho interesante sobre estos animales es _____

50 Fun-Filled Spanish Draw & Write Prompts Scholastic Professional Books

Cómo dibujar un murciélago

Nombre _____

Sigue los pasos para dibujar un murciélago.
Dibuja tu murciélago en el recuadro de la página siguiente.

Paso 1

Paso 2

Paso 3

Paso 4

Paso 5

Paso 6

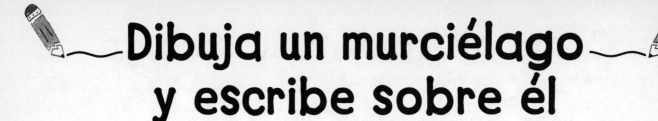

Dibuja un murciélago
y escribe sobre él

por _____

Dibuja tu murciélago en el recuadro de abajo.

Había una vez un murciélago llamado _____.

Vivía en un/a _____.

_____ y le gustaba hacer muchas cosas.

Le gustaba _____.

Pero, había una cosa que no le gustaba hacer.

No le gustaba _____.

Por eso, en lugar de eso él _____.

50 Fun-Filled Spanish Draw & Write Prompts Scholastic Professional Books

Cómo dibujar
un pulpo

Nombre _____

Sigue estos pasos para dibujar un pulpo.
Dibuja tu pulpo en el recuadro de la página siguiente.

Paso 1	**Paso 2**
Paso 3	**Paso 4**
Paso 5	**Paso 6**

Dibuja un pulpo y escribe sobre él

por _____

Dibuja tu pulpo en el recuadro de abajo.

Había una vez un pulpo llamado _____.

Estaba cansado de vivir en el océano.

Quería vivir en _____.

Todos los días se _____.

Finalmente, el pulpo decidió _____.

Eso lo hizo sentirse _____.

50 Fun-Filled Spanish Draw & Write Prompts Scholastic Professional Books

Cómo dibujar
una jirafa

Nombre _____

Sigue los pasos para dibujar una jirafa.
Dibuja tu jirafa en el recuadro de la página siguiente.

Paso 1	Paso 2
Paso 3	Paso 4
Paso 5	Paso 6

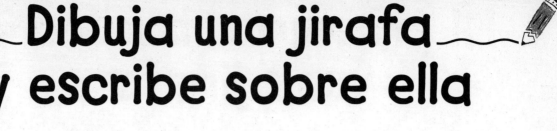

Dibuja una jirafa
y escribe sobre ella

por _____

Dibuja tu jirafa en el recuadro de abajo.

Había una vez una jirafa llamada _____.

La jirafa se preguntaba siempre por qué tenía un cuello tan largo.

Entonces, le preguntó a un sabio _____.

El sabio _____ dijo que las jirafas tenían cuellos largos

porque _____

_____.

62

Mi criatura imaginaria

por _____

Este es el dibujo de mi criatura imaginaria.

¿Cómo se llama tu criatura? _____

¿De qué color es? _____

¿Cuán grande es? _____

¿Qué come? _____

¿Qué cosas especiales puede hacer? _____

La historia de mi criatura imaginaria

por _____

El título de mi historia es _____

En los recuadros de abajo, dibuja cuatro cosas que le ocurrieron a tu criatura. Luego escribe sobre eso en las líneas.

1

_____
_____

2

_____
_____

3

_____
_____

4

_____
_____

50 Fun-Filled Spanish Draw & Write Prompts Scholastic Professional Books